The Peddler
AND THE PRESIDENT

By Ann Diament Koffsky   Illustrated by Pedro Rodríguez

For my Israeli family: David, Adina, Yoni, Sefi, Eliana, Dovi, plus Ilana, and the rest of the extended *mishpachah*.
—ADK

In honor of the Sephardi people.
—PR

The publisher wishes to thank the Harry S. Truman Presidential Library and Museum staff for their generous time and assistance.

Apples & Honey Press
An Imprint of Behrman House Publishers
Millburn, New Jersey 07041
www.applesandhoneypress.com

ISBN 978-1-68115-637-8

Text copyright © 2025 by Ann D. Koffsky
Illustrations copyright © 2025 by Pedro Rodríguez

All rights reserved. No part of this publication may be translated, reproduced, stored in a retrieval system or transmitted, in any form or by any means, electronic, mechanical, photocopying, recording or otherwise, for any purpose, without express written permission from the publishers.

Library of Congress Cataloging-in-Publication Data

Names: Koffsky, Ann Diament, author. | Rodríguez, Pedro, 1973- illustrator.
Title: The peddler and the president / by Ann Diament Koffsky ; illustrated by Pedro Rodriguez.
Description: Millburn : Apples & Honey Press, 2025. | Includes bibliographical references and index. |
Audience: Ages 6-9 | Audience: Grades 2-3 | Summary: "The true story of the friendship between Harry Truman and Eddie Jacobson"—Provided by publisher.
Identifiers: LCCN 2024022684 | ISBN 9781681156378 (hardcover)
Subjects: LCSH: Truman, Harry S., 1884-1972—Friends and associates—Juvenile literature. | Jacobson, Edward, 1891-1955—Juvenile literature. | Zionists—United States—Biography—Juvenile literature. | United States—Foreign relations—United States—Juvenile literature. | Palestine—Foreign relations—United States—Juvenile literature. | Israel—History—1948-1967—Juvenile literature. Classification: LCC E814 .K644 2025 | DDC 973.918092 [B]—dc23/eng/20240823 LC record available at https://lccn.loc.gov/2024022684

Art direction and design by Elynn Cohen
Edited by Aviva Lucas Gutnick
Printed in China

1 3 5 7 9 8 6 4 2

Lexile ® 710L

CONTENTS

★ ★ ★ ★ ★ ★ ★ ★ ★ ★ ★

CHAPTER 1: New Friends 1

CHAPTER 2: New Partners 7

CHAPTER 3: New Jobs 13

CHAPTER 4: New President 19

CHAPTER 5: New Hope 29

CHAPTER 6: New Country 37

EPILOGUE: Old Friends 45

Timeline 47

Author's Note 48

NEW FRIENDS
1903

Most people who saw Harry and Eddie would have been surprised they were friends.

Harry was twenty-two.

Eddie was fifteen.

Harry lived on a farm with chickens, cows, and horses.

Eddie never even had a pet.

Harry was Christian.

Eddie was Jewish.

But Harry and Eddie had something important in common. They had both stopped going to school so they could work and help their struggling families.

Harry worked at the biggest bank in Kansas City.

Eddie worked at a busy dry goods store just a few short blocks away. It sold things like clothing, fabric, flour, coffee, and sugar.

Every day, Eddie collected the money from the store's cash register. Then he would walk to the bank, open its heavy doors, and put the money on Harry's desk.

Harry and Eddie would chat and swap stories while Harry deposited the money in the store's account.

A year later, Harry left Kansas City to work on his family's farm.

Eddie missed Harry.

Harry missed Eddie.

But they each grew too busy to write letters or visit one another.

They lost touch.

NEW PARTNERS
1914-1917

World War I had begun in Europe. Three years later, the United States entered the fighting. It was one of the deadliest wars in human history, and every soldier was needed. Harry joined the army.

The army sent Harry to a base in Oklahoma for training, and when he got there, he couldn't believe it. Eddie was there too! They shook hands warmly, thrilled to see each other again.

"Truman! Jacobson! I'm putting you in charge of the canteen, the army store," ordered the head officer.

"YES SIR!" they saluted.

Together Harry and Eddie went to look at the store. Right away they saw problems. The store sold few things soldiers would want to buy. It didn't even have a cash register. There were just beat-up cardboard boxes for the soldiers to put their money inside.

Harry and Eddie worked hard to make it into the best store it could be. They bought a cash register. They filled the store with things soldiers wanted: soda, candy, writing paper, and more. They even added a barber and a tailor, so that soldiers could get their hair cut and their clothing fixed—and buy things—all in one place.

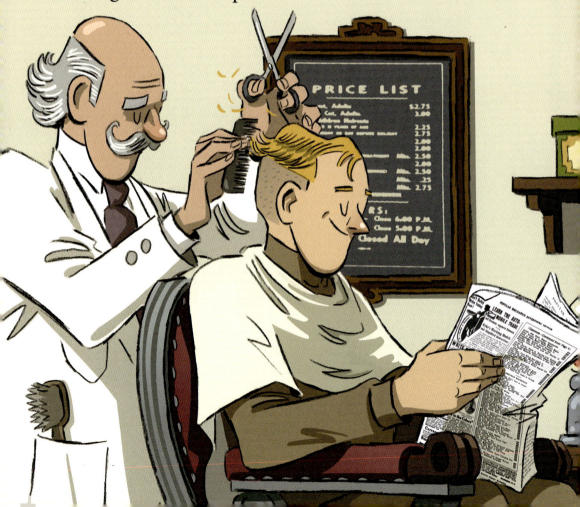

Harry and Eddie loved working together on the store, and the soldiers loved shopping there. It made more money than ever before and was a huge success. Then they both were sent to fight the war in Europe, and didn't see each other until after it ended.

NEW JOBS

1918-1945

When the war ended, Harry and Eddie left the army and had to find new jobs. Since they had liked working together so much, they decided to team up again and open a hat store. They put their names on the store: Truman & Jacobson Haberdashery.

At first, people loved that store too. But when hard times came, people didn't have enough money to buy hats. The store failed, and once again Harry and Eddie needed to find jobs.

Eddie became a salesman. He traveled a lot. He knocked on doors and sold pajamas. He would come home to his wife, Bluma, and his daughters, Elinor and Gloria. Together they would go to temple on Saturday. Eventually, after a lot of hard work and many jobs along the way, Eddie was able to open his own clothing store in Kansas City.

Harry became a politician and also traveled a lot. He knocked on doors and asked people to vote for him. He would come home to his wife, Bess, and his daughter, Margaret. Together, they would visit their family farm on Sundays. Eventually, after a lot of hard work and many jobs along the way, Harry was elected vice president of the United States alongside President Franklin Delano Roosevelt.

Harry and Eddie were both very busy, and they missed each other.

So Harry and Eddie stayed in touch. They made sure to visit each other whenever they could. Sometimes they would meet at Eddie's house to play cards or music, go fishing on the Missouri River, or meet up at Dixon's Chili Parlor for some ribs.

But they never met at Harry's house. Harry's wife, Bess, wouldn't let Eddie into her house.

Eddie and his family could not understand it. They hadn't done anything wrong. They wondered if Bess didn't like Jews. It was hard to know.

But Bess was in charge of the house, and Harry didn't want to argue with her. He stayed quiet.

Eddie was very hurt. But he didn't want to argue with Harry. He stayed quiet too.

NEW PRESIDENT
1945

We interrupt this program to bring you a special news bulletin. President Roosevelt is dead. Vice President Harry S. Truman is now president of the United States.

Eddie went with his family to temple to pray for President Roosevelt's family and for the new president of the United States, his old friend Harry.

Salesmen and presidents aren't usually best friends. But Harry and Eddie were.

Harry continued to visit Eddie whenever he could. When Eddie opened a clothing store in Kansas City, Harry made sure to stop in and buy some shirts. The whole town was surprised to see the president of the United States shopping. It made headlines in the newspaper.

Eddie also visited Harry whenever he could. Eddie would fly to Washington, DC, and ride to the White House. Even if he didn't have an appointment, the White House staff would always let Eddie walk right into Harry's Oval Office. There, the two friends would talk.

Some of Eddie's friends told him, "You should ask the president for a job! Or tickets to a ball game!"

But Eddie just shook his head. He didn't want anything from Harry except his friendship. So he stayed quiet.

Harry's job meant making hard decisions, and in 1948 he had to make one about a place far from the United States.

Thousands of years earlier, the Jewish people lived in a land they called Eretz Yisrael. But in the year 70 CE, the Roman army forced most of them to leave

their homeland. The Romans later renamed the land "Palestine." Ever since, many Jews had been hoping to return.

They especially hoped so now. World War II had ended just after Harry became president. During the war, it had been very dangerous to be Jewish in Europe, and many Jews had been murdered. With the war over, thousands of Jews who had survived had nowhere safe to live. Many wanted to move to their ancient homeland and make it into a new country where they could be safe and free.

Would kings, prime ministers, and presidents from around the world support a modern Jewish country?

NEW HOPE
1947

One of the Jewish leaders working for a new country was Dr. Chaim Weizmann. He traveled around the world to meet with kings, prime ministers, and presidents and asked them to say, "Yes! We support a new Jewish country in the land of Palestine!"

Rabbis, like the one from Eddie's temple in Missouri, made speeches asking them to say, "Yes!"

Mothers, fathers, and schoolchildren all around the country wrote letters to Harry asking him to say, "Yes!"

They all hoped that if the president of the United States said that he supported creating a new Jewish country in Palestine, then the rest of the world would too.

But just like Bess didn't want Jews inside her home, there were also people who didn't want Jews to have their own homeland. Several countries even threatened to start a war if a new Jewish country was made.

Some of Harry's advisers were scared. They didn't want another war, so they advised Harry to keep quiet.

But the letters to Harry kept piling up. Soon there were thousands of them.

Each one asked Harry over and over to "say yes to a Jewish country!"

Harry's advisers asked him over and over to "keep quiet!"

Finally Harry lost his patience. He shouted to his staff that he would not talk about a Jewish country in Palestine anymore to anyone. He refused to read any more letters. He refused to talk about it with his advisers or to meet with anyone about it.

Jewish leaders were scared. If the president wouldn't even meet with the well-respected Dr. Chaim Weizmann, Harry might say, "No!" And if the president of the United States said "no," other world leaders might copy him and also say, "No, we won't support a new Jewish country."

As a last hope, one leader called Eddie for help.

Briinnnggg!!

Who's calling me in the middle of the night?! Eddie wondered.

"You must convince the president to see Dr. Weizmann!" Eddie heard when he picked up the phone.

Eddie hung up and closed his eyes. *I've never asked Harry for anything,* he thought. *I don't want Harry to think I'm friends with him just to get things from him.*

But then he thought some more. . . .

Across the ocean, children just like my Elinor and Gloria have nowhere to go. They need a safe home.

He knew that *now* was the time to speak. This was too important to stay quiet.

Eddie started packing and got on a plane.

NEW COUNTRY
1948

On March 12, 1948, Eddie walked through the front gate of the White House. He didn't have an appointment, but he knew that he would be allowed into the Oval Office to see his old friend, just like always.

"Mr. Jacobson, you can go right in," said the man at the desk. "Just please: don't talk with the president about Palestine! He doesn't want to discuss that with anyone, anymore."

Eddie opened the door and walked into the Oval Office. He could feel his heart beating hard. His hands shook. He felt more nervous than he had ever felt before.

Harry could tell.

"Eddie, what in the world is the matter with you?" Harry asked, shaking hands with Eddie and taking his seat behind the presidential desk.

Eddie took a deep breath. It was time for him to stop staying quiet.

"You must see Dr. Weizmann," Eddie said. "You must support an independent Jewish state."

Harry's face turned red, and his fists clenched. Eddie kept talking. "Dr. Weizmann traveled thousands and thousands of miles just to see you! Now you refuse to see him? It doesn't sound like you, Harry."

Harry turned away. He drummed his fingers on the arm of his chair. He was thinking hard about a tough decision.

Eddie could tell.

For a long time, it was very quiet. Finally, Harry spun back and looked at his friend. "You win!" Harry said angrily. "I will see him."

Soon after, Dr. Chaim Weizmann met with the president of the United States. They talked about the Jewish people's hope to return to their ancient homeland, about how they had suffered during World War II, and about all the children who needed a safe home.

After their meeting, Harry didn't stay quiet. He told the world, "Yes, the United States supports a new Jewish country."

And on May 14, 1948, when the Jews in Palestine declared the creation of the State of Israel, many countries around the world followed Harry's example. They also said, "Yes, we support the creation of Israel." Later they voted to make Israel a full member of the United Nations.

Jewish people everywhere celebrated. Eddie and his family celebrated.

Israel was no longer just a hope. It was real.

Two good friends had helped make it so.

And for the rest of their lives, Harry and Eddie stayed the best of friends.

EPILOGUE
OLD FRIENDS

In 1952, President Harry Truman chose not to run for re-election. He moved back to his home in Missouri, close to where Eddie lived. Once again, Harry and Eddie started getting together regularly to fish, hunt, and play cards. They even started to plan a big vacation and hoped to visit many countries together: England, the Netherlands, Greece, Turkey—and Israel.

Unfortunately, they never got to take their trip, because Eddie had a heart attack and died on October 25, 1955.

After Eddie's funeral, the former president of the United States visited the Jacobson family as they sat shiva for Eddie. Together they mourned and cried over their loss of Eddie. Later Truman said, "I don't think I've ever known a man I thought more of, outside my own family, than I did of Eddie Jacobson. He's one of the finest men that ever walked on this earth."

*Eddie Jacobson (left) and Harry Truman (right), 1954.
Photo courtesy of Harry S. Truman Library.*

TIMELINE

70 The Roman Empire destroys the Second Temple in Jerusalem, forcing many Jews into exile from Eretz Yisrael. Many are forced into slavery and marched to Rome.

135 Rome renames Eretz Yisrael as Palestine.

1914-1918 World War I. Eddie Jacobson and Harry Truman are both sent to France to fight.

1919 Eddie and Harry are both sent home to the United States, where they reconnect and discuss going into business together.

1939-1945 World War II.

1945 Vice President Truman becomes the thirty-third president of the United States upon the death of President Franklin Roosevelt.

November 29, 1947 United Nations recommends the establishment of separate Arab and Jewish states in Palestine, then under control of Britain.

March 18, 1948 President Truman meets with Dr. Chaim Weizmann in secret at the White House.

May 14, 1948 Israel declares independence. Eleven minutes later, President Truman recognizes Israel.

May 11, 1949 Israel is admitted to the United Nations as a full member.

May 25, 1948 Weizmann, now the first president of Israel, presents a Torah to President Truman on a visit to the White House.

March 29, 1952 Truman announces he will not run for reelection.

October 25, 1955 Eddie Jacobson dies.

December 26, 1972 Harry Truman dies.

AUTHOR'S NOTE

Dear Reader,

Harry and Eddie's friendship was remarkable in so many ways, beginning when they were young men and lasting through the challenges of a war, a failed business partnership, and one of them becoming the most powerful person in the country.

But what I find most inspiring about their friendship was their respect for each other.

Even though the president of the United States was his best friend, Eddie respected their friendship too much to ask Harry for any favors or special treatment. Not until the stakes were so high did Eddie know he had to speak up. That made Eddie's request all the more powerful. Harry knew that Eddie would never ask for anything unless it was incredibly important.

Harry too respected their friendship, so much that he was willing to hear Eddie out and really listen. In the weeks before Eddie marched into the White House, President Truman met with many of his expert advisors who strongly cautioned him to stay silent on Israel. Only Harry Truman's deep respect for Eddie allowed him to listen, and ultimately change his mind.

Their mutual love and respect led them to change the world.

Ann